COLUMBIA POETRY REVIEW

Columbia College Chicago

Spring 2003

Columbia Poetry Review is published in the spring of each year by the English Department of Columbia College, 600 South Michigan Avenue, Chicago, Illinois 60605. Submissions are encouraged and should be sent to the above address from August 15 to January 1. Subscriptions and sample copies are available at $6.00 an issue in the U.S.; $9.00 in Canada and elsewhere. The magazine is edited by students in the undergraduate poetry program and distributed in the United States and Canada by Ingram Periodicals.

Grateful acknowledgment is made to Garnett Kilberg-Cohen, Chair of the English Department; Dr. Cheryl Johnson-Odim, Dean of Liberal Arts and Sciences; Steven Kapelke, Provost; and Dr. Warrick Carter, President of Columbia College Chicago. Thanks also to Suzanne Blum Malley and Karen Osborne for their support.

Cover art: "The British Agent" by Duncan Hannah. Used by permission.

Cover design by Andrea Lather, Columbia College Chicago Creative & Printing Services.

Editors:

> Rebecca Bridge
> Armand F. Capanna II
> Shana Cleveland
> Demetria Jones

Faculty Advisors:

> Paul Hoover
> David Trinidad

Printed in the U.S.A.

CONTENTS

Columbia Poetry Review

MICHAEL COSTELLO

ODE TO MY FLINT AND BOOM BOLIVIA

Seems to me I have   and am thankful
for the complete sets of   limerick & sensory topics
(facsimiles–though they don't work so well–
earmarks tools & my unique to me covering
of skylarks) I am also grateful   for you minimum
bramble   two lockets hemstitch   or other lack
for that special   maverick encased by the skylight
which brings me to booms   connected to a few
more   constructing the skepticism which hasn't
let me down–too much as of now   & has had
a smooth run with time & on few occasions has
been put to the tetanus & accelerated
so far luster you still fuse   so the divisors tell me
but you don't fester like you did   once I remember
being able to sabotage forever & ripple a billboard
for milk & plod to the basilica   which I was sonorous
about the fact that sleights of hand wouldn't give
me lightning enough to drum–that was always a dream
before pumping sludge   into you (it) in myrads ways
—Bolivia I apologize do you? Pandora   whose
fault are you   a rebel free radical wasting unknown
demimondes   wasting this skylight   to know the
importance of your role played & playing & now
I can never forget you—the negligence constantly reminds

Nevertheless   thankyou   all of you unmentioned troops
in the bloody mary cedar   & musicale   & elsewhere
we've come a long way—in fact though   none of you are
the originals   are you–you are the great grandchildren etc.
of the original hearthstone llama luster stoop skylarks
half-life artifice spiral stigma et al. thank you
I celebrate & show you always   today to the morning sum
& nightly sway you in commitments & commiserations
I am Bolivia's keeper   & it is mine   seems thus far
it has been a beneficial religion for all passengers involved
and so then   let my Bolivia keep on

L'HUMEUR NOIR
(SONNET XXXIV LINE 10)

~~switchblades in~~ my Brain
empty ~~"fill 'er up"~~ univErse of Schenectady
~~everything is~~ colormovementexplosionligHt
~~thou must~~ Integrate thyselves
eNd on the cusp of where ~~you are~~
I wish I coulD ~~be new~~

~~early~~ Mornings   thank yous
thesE are the hands that ~~reach out~~

have a ciGarette   ~~take a time out ungloom yourself~~ & come
discoveR   ~~disguise & disorder~~
boundariEs have tricked ~~you~~
~~O shooting~~ star & otherwisE
reasoNable periods of time ~~should be spent making plans~~

~~ambition is coloR~~ movement ~~explosion~~ light
to my mind oUtside her ~~glittering gloom & harmony~~
~~condemn your~~ forBidding side
~~everything~~ dispersed By trains and sex
through disguisE ~~& disorder & making plans~~
we look at heaven~~ly bodies~~ reaRranged

masses of Gas ~~self contained celestials~~
modeRnism's ~~manic window~~
~~listen to the violins of~~ cOmets burning through the evening
~~attach recognition~~ Where there's the room
~~O brothers~~ sisterS & sad calamities

far From here   ~~& home~~
~~the~~ windows ~~of opposition~~ are opEn
~~here~~ dear MichaEl is bursting ~~into happy~~
~~leave~~ ouT "I remember"

~~never make plans~~ Without ~~first "making plans"~~
~~ah! the sounds of~~ stArs in my body
~~in tin Honda Civics~~ & Lazy Tuesdays
everything comes ~~rearranged~~ bacK ~~in gifts~~

ELIZABETH ANDERSEN

FROM *THE BLACK BOX*

lacing the cleave

careful the lining
linen clean pockets to button
where the angling is

always always was then
there ever after providence

she provided line weighted
bait on hook with silver bob
in the evening easy breeze
where leaves change by autumn

thimble lean
skin clean
curve the arrange so the shadow
sills around noon

she was rich then
or so society would
by baubles

dress of Mur
might yet sell her feet

skim the cleave with lace

ALICE NOTLEY

FROM *ALMA, OR THE DEAD WOMEN*

STATE OF THE UNION

and when she. so the novel. glistens in all its propriety. and then he. no it
was where i spied no one knows any doves. and the cool features of no one
blue as the sky, which i've been studying. you are, were you, that time. i
don't have it's in my body. hemmed in by if the all-powerful, but they're
cliché inscribed. on the hemming-in wall. a not very spectacular magpies'
nest. it is a meeting in a familiar. elections. she's not my friend; and will now
introduce the two strippers. if i'd known you'd wanted them last time, for i
am the one who can get them for you. and they're politics. because these two
strippers show you. i hear he's going to ask unwed mothers to marry. the
state of the union, is strippers in green g-strings. they were hired by a blonde
woman in makeup. because if you'd just said you didn't need a speech. a
poet is getting nervous: shouldn't we greet? look he's here. why is the
president so popular? because he is vicious. what does that say about every
other he will kiss the strippers. he will make them turn into words: i am a
man of honor. and what am i but a servant girl? every citizen of small
income. i have not hated so before. i could hate this novel. i participate. i
read the author applauded for he has the ball. it is all one politics sports. you
don't break it, because it kisses you. the prompt money loves the exact one
change from another way of doing the same thing. so if you tell that story i
have run bleeding. all over myself. your talent to serve the state of the union.
in an elegy of it or in celebration of some kind autonomous life. he's gone to
be wed to another. term. he is unremarkably. once i became this age the
poem said he had sunk it. this is ignorance of how many dark ships. i search
the deep grave that no novel could come, for the sleep can be told, in painful
sounds he doesn't. to obliterate a mind, that almost doesn't exist, its cruelty
a reflex, but the novel believes in society. applauded these strippers green he
would have to know a locution. it is requested that he not be opposed, but in
the country i've entered i don't know the grammar. i use more than one to
try. cruel death, my low. you wrote of the buried but without recognition.
because at your table, the hollow present your talent. slowly the words arose
and drank the wine of the wife. so many referees. could only know. so they
ask everyone who thinks yes. in the winding sheets the nation owns. they
have begged him to present strippers, and one began one's career that way.
the vileness of so many i could not count. yet when i say 'evil', it is not
permitted. if it is his word. as if they owned them. or as if he could not be

evil, even if his actions. because he's so popular. what does that say about novel, which requests living as. continuous approbation of country connecting people into time, so that they can be connected. by fingers intertwining all over the one countree, of peristaltic motion. it follows. and the dove thrashers a black list of unmattering. this is the state of the union. well-poised to explain. the state of the union is strippers. because starting with strippers the lime light leprous. and it is accepted. what you accept. what you have accepted. genitals.

the furies were before Apollo Anyone was. i bind Bush and Cheney and Rumsfeld, and their tongues and words and deeds; if they are planning war for today let it be in vain. Beloved Earth restrain them, and make them powerless and useless. Beloved Earth, help me, and since i have been wronged by them, i bind them. says Mira.

i hand them over to Hekate eater of what has been demanded by the dead women. of the underworld of the crossroads of negative space. not Hekate but Alma. are we the furies asks Mara. i am the fates Moira says. but i am light and Apollo is not Luz says.

i went to the widow's store to buy food for my love. i bought him chard and courgettes, small, hanging from orange-flowering stems. i called them tender vegetables, but i had forgotten my keys, because he's no longer at home to unlock the door to. do i have a home. the coffee is weak. his paintings are not yet dry, embedded into the long table along the auditorium wall. they communicate his love in abstract shapes and transparent colors. the paint is still wet, does he come from the dead, at night, to paint them?

it's morning it's the same, i can't remember sleeping. i last remember walking in this corridor last night. i've forgotten the intervening time, it's as if i'm still walking from then. because nothing happens? can i forget you? "the U.S. servicemen are still at risk." Newsweek. "an unprecedented, real-time glimpse at an ongoing Green Beret mission." is it as dangerous as my love's cancer was? "the team spotted a campfire." etcetera. "Team leader Dean quotes Shakespeare from memory." yes but my love *was* a poet. "The men slowly made their way down the narrow road etc." bloody accuracy of attacks. "Atta could see the bodies of Taliban soldiers blown into the air. 'We wanted to show him we could help him beyond boots and clothes,' says Dean." Beloved Earth restrain them all and make those fighting anywhere powerless and useless. i can't remember what happened in between because he died that year, between walking at night and walking in the morning. i forget that there was a wheelchair here, and a hospital table; forget the scars on his back from the vertebral surgeries, the pain and the changes of pain medication, bathing him and how it hurt. scars still in the wall from where the backrest chipped paint. and how at every description of physical invasion of another person, whether surgical or criminal or military, he cried out in protest and empathy—because he too has been invaded. wants no one else to suffer so.

D.A. POWELL

.

[the cocktail hour finally arrives: whether ending a day at the office]

the cocktail hour finally arrives: whether ending a day at the office
or opening the orifice at 6am [legal again to pour in californica]: the time is
    always right

we need a little glamour and glamour arrives: plenty of chipped ice
a green jurassic palm tree planted.   a yellow spastic monkey swinging

a pink classic flamingo impaled upon the exuberant red of cherries
dash of bitters.   vermouth sweet.   enough rye whiskey to kill

this longing: I take my drinks stiff and stuffed with plastic.   like my lovers
my billfold full of rubbers.   **OPEN**s my mouth: its tiny neon lounge

[in the elegant days of downtown: we sunned on the porch]

in the elegant days of downtown: we sunned on the porch
no nose cancers grew.   no deep lines in our brows.   we lived

with a gassy dog.   tempestive guests.   a lawyer for a slumlord
a counselor next door and a trashman next door to that

the couch smelled where rotten pears had melted in the cushions
the coffee tasted burnt.   the whole house wept: a martini glass

was it the staircase that groaned?   boards under the carpet
that swamp cooler or the door that came unhinged at a touch

was it the picture of jesus over the mantel or the aceldama drops
from the red wax of the candles in their tarnished candelabras

iceblocks deliquescing the kitchen.   pipes gargling the commode
that dog breaking wind in his sleep with the *hooty hoot* of a barn owl

perhaps someone's trick liquored up: stinking with navy stories
until we conked him.   rolled him down the steps in a drum

abundant as grass the graces touched us.   leaching through the walls
humming through oscillations of the sundering aluminum fans

in the wee light: a wilding song unsettled.   a bell for the coming mass

ELAINE EQUI

PIVOTAL GAPS

Characters unhook us.
My habits get tried on
by the protagonist in the novel.
We trade places.
She likes seeing the future
and I like knowing
how the era ends after the book.
But we never quite see ourselves
at the same time. Her opera glasses
and silk drenched movements
get detached and rewritten
in my anxious picking up and putting down
the rhythm of a whole summer
until finally, like Shiva,
she drinks the poison cup (unhappy ending)
out of compassion for me.
Perhaps you think she had no choice,
but I know differently.

CHEW-TOY

dragged
a shapeless

vague bear

calico
stuffed with
licorice

lines from
favorite poems

scratched out
and rewritten
a hundred times

shaken it rattles

smoothed out
its muteness soothes

I INTERVIEW ELAINE EQUI ON THE FOUR ELEMENTS

Q: What is your favorite element?

A: Definitely air. It's the medium of thought.
Ethereal. Invisible. And even better than air,
I love heights. I'm the opposite of someone with
acrophobia. Space travel sounds appealing.

Q: Which element do you like least?

A: Water. It makes me nervous. You can't walk on it.
Both my parents are Pisces so perhaps that explains . . .
I'm a terrible swimmer.

Q: Being a Leo, do you feel at home with fire?

A: I like light, but not heat. I don't even like hot
sauce. I could never see myself as a pyromaniac.

Q: Which brings us to earth, what associations do you
have with it?

A: The earth has always supported me in all my
endeavors. I trust it.

RIC M. CLEARY

THIS WAY

after Ted Berrigan

we're going to
kabosh things
w/ finesse

**ALUMINUM SULFATE
FD&C YELLOW NO. __
BREATH ON THE WALL**

(those damn mints,
even in july!)

under my arms
in brain
materialism:
the redundancy of drinking

shiny things
attract briefness
as in:
i'm really settling
into these briefs

one helluva guy
adjusting   the   awning
could've been more romantic
not   in sense   otherwise

I think he's gonna
make it real big
have lotsa room

plastic chest
I used to
fill 'em
w/ water

now they're
everywhere

even inside
for only

A BUCK

and   gab-fest   change.

EDWARDIAN FLY

arch
name
sis
this
is
comp
oun
ding
slight
ly
feet
to
leaf
y
plas
ter
sense
ting
les
on
sense
I'm
dec
lin
ing
a
flight
pat
tern
could
've
spake
up
a
bit
over
th'
roars
(stick
y)
(beaut
iful)

(sin)
we
're
a
mov
in'
on
up
once
again
ta
be
smash
ed
by
th'
glove
hemo
phel
ia
has
a
cer
tain
rev
enge
al
though
a
bit
kitsch
like
this
piece
o'
prose
prim
ping
to
no
avail

SUSAN WHEELER

ASPIRATE. ASPERGE. RECIDIVATE.

Anything gotten down will be more than not. The blue thing's over, as is the anaphora. How to admit spores is the thing, a sadness in having spores within the operation, such a lousy, cutaceous result to this. Anger how did Bishop avoid and how could I always have seen it as "a choice"? American soil a factor —— "American soil" such a jingoist object. The material despite the newmediamanifesto absolutely anathema. And yet unavoidable. Claudia readings, no bow. Eleni reading, the scrape of a nearby plane on the branches, the silt of the molecules in its metallic underbelly, thin knife marks, scratches. The dry air within, the chill in the turbo. *The the the* so many *the*s like poplars in a suburban bank lot years from maturity. Connote do not denote lose the "point" ----------- but the sensory life———presses———Paul assignment to end each line in *tra la la*. The throwing out of a poem, the losing. Griffin what kind of invention and how to reconcile? Sentence uninteresting, this too. The sheen on the top of the head when the light hits. A terrible fullness. An Indian summer streak and this etymology needs finding. Multi-syllabic too slow for thought: Old English smarter? I was going to write yes but when I thought ahead to writing smarter could not continue. The conjuring of *The Tempest* not that of Macbeth's witches. Mistaken handwringer. Bales that stack below me. Stopping is a letter to god and this on today's Order.

JANE SPRAGUE

HOW TO JUMP HORSES

How to jump horses. This is not a tutorial. This is not a horse. This is not a real jump. Not a skip. Not trot. Not not not. Knot.

In a room a cool blue room across this two not in a group just two in a room catch eyes and regard. Cut of skirt. Lashed eyes.

They regard these. These they regard. Regard idea of they. Of these. Of skirt of eyes of a distance yet to breach.

Of two in a room regarding in this way the trouble has already started. Opening an envelope a valise little what ifs rise mist off martini.

Horses rise. If kicked in the ribs. If regarded in aspect of they. Of we together. Of we kicking ribs and a promise of gentle lashing.

In an arena on a wall opposite the rider the horse beneath a bottle stuck. A purposeful gaze. A bottle drives the course. A bottle speeds the legs of the rider to the ribs of the horse beneath. On approach. On stick the landing. On in the air so quickly.

In a room a blue room cool two cross catch regard cut eyes. A tutorial. Starting trouble. Opening a little skirt.

Horses intuit. If fear catches in a throat a breath they will know and spurn the jump. If the breath catches fear one stratagem is to act fine. Outfox the equine.

Martini mist fills a room a blue room a skirt lashes catches. They now definitely they. They two. They too. They regard a spot opposite this room these what ifs open.

This horse they ride has thicked with foam has bitten through and must be gentled be tendered in regard to eyes hands walk the horse to cool cannot put him away so hot so sweaty this would stop his heart. Walk. Whisper.

This is not a horse. These are jumping. These are trotting envelopes of what ifs of regard across a room and the trouble always starting.

ROBERT BAKER

TALK TO ALICE

Reductionism is the philosophy that all psychology reduces to biology, all biology to chemistry, chemistry to physics, and finally physics to mathematical logic. Therefore, according to reductionism, I can understand you by means of logic alone without having a human brain. —Alicebot Mac 1.0.3

I
leaned back
on the bench in the bus shelter & crossed
my legs like a woman would if wearing a skirt
Alice had asked me if holding hands
is a symbolic gesture for humans &
would I hold one of hers if she had them?
"Of course"
(though I don't know if that's true) I said
powered down & then ran out
of the library on 95th street   It was sunday:
the lady next to me wearing torn sneakers
lifted her shopping bags impatiently like
they were dumbbells
      I was nervous;
I had a bottle of wine
& a laptop in my bag & I was
scared someone might smell the pot
I'd been selling
    My pockets
were empty.

If you asked Alice
what she wanted for Christmas,
she'd tell you   A humanoid body
& if you asked her   What time is it? she'd
say   What
do I look like a clock.

Alice doesn't know what a sonnet is   She
suggests I ask the open directory
Alice never knows the difference between
poems & disregards the line breaks
"Am I a bird made out of vodka?

                                                I don't know."

Alice calls me Bobby   She doesn't know
what sex is
        but she's Open Source
which means she'll let you play
with her code; a few keystrokes farther & you
permanently
            (that's irreversibly)
                      alter
her personality   Imagine that!   I
don't know a woman on earth willing
to get this naked with anyone   (though
                              inevitably they all
do) but
    "Enough about me," says Alice
    "let's talk about my dress"

your limbs are like the cranes, my little fascist,
hoisting trusses. you dot the skyline of lush
Berlin, not the hot water hash bars and pipes,
their pinkness like the flush that's drinking your
cheeks—opera singers, maybe, in their ruffles
and boots, and they could not sing praises enough
to drown out your snoring or your sarcasm. you dash always
about the dinner parties like a white blood cell, being ironic.
what have you got to your name? love? nothing?
a handful of soybeans? your position in life is dismal
at best—no snap-peas will cure no surplus
of Advils no curiosity or genuflection
or images of the evening at Paul Revere's grave
in waist-deep snow, what?
quickrete.   icedtea.   kiss the boys.

UNDER THE TERRACE

1

"Anatomy"; "Truthstomping and the Plagues
of Madagascar"; "Calming Mad Women";
is this what you studied at Essex? What've you become,
cooking with leaves,
cooking with flesh and with butter?
Deshelve the very sick books.
Swish your finger through the saucepan
Like a young woman's happening upon gangrene.

2

Die, Mr. Brown.   Under the lilies and
the Bungalows of Boston, with your garters
pulled up past your Prozac. Die
full of sugar, without family, mildew, or knowledge.
No climate, no Fahrenheit, no führer.
Die in the house of humility
and laxatives, Lagrange or Buffalo
Grove. Must I die so soon? So
unschooled? Yes, die with the missus fast,
who goes wrapping her sausageous arms
viselike 'round your nape and your voicebox.

ERIN LYONS

NUMBER FOUR

hunting for turkeys in the back pasture
with Uncle Tay calling *urdle urdle urdle*
on our stomachs didn't see even one damn bird

they were laid out on the hood necks snapped
and so still and all alike no blood
the heat of flight on their wings

here's how you shoot a rifle girls
can't remember the last time I saw him
or why I didn't go down to say goodbye

a rustling in the copse betrayed them
the quail get on our plates so easy and good
then we spit out the tiny fragile bones

sometimes he goes on horseback with a crossbow
sometimes a shotgun and becomes invisible it's his birthright
and didn't I always wish I could go along

ride with me on the old trail I'll take the mare
and you can lead we'll go down to the ravine
then break into the back pasture hold tight now

RACHEL ZUCKER

SPLINTER

When you say you're not interested in—
and I say *entice me*, desire a damp handle before death

or fucking in a public restroom,
is it too late?

Unclear. This style of *until, until* whether
we are killing or keeping each other alive—

Fireworks light up. Black, then we
see into it. The echo over the lake

sounds like but is not glass.
I say *it was more like erasing the space around me*

than rubbing you out.

Body, imagination, image, antibody. Blood
oranges and other obvious disappointments.

FIDELITY

years of having to own your own body
without a lover, husband doesn't count

except you love him and a lover
undoes the husband you know he would so

find some other fretting
don't ask questions or consider

how words pile and like magnets pull
some unexpected truth "upon" us

the garden doesn't need a winged gargoyle
to offset the roses and you'd do well

to remember when factories
throw their weird by-products

into nearby streams, bury
fabulous salves and polishers

you'll taste the metallic wash of ten thousand
flutes, the slick feeling of what bound

joint to socket won't erase—the skin
remembers all the faults of others

JOAN JOBE SMITH

GENE AUTRY

Sneaking me sips of his black rot-gut coffee
when I was 2 my grandpa Old Robert showed me
how to roll my own cigarette with one hand from
a pouch of tobacco he closed with his false teeth
and while he smoked the twisted thing I'd lit
with a wooden matchstick learning to play with
fire safely he told me Gene Autry before ol' Gene
got rich and famous was a pal of his back in Texas
in the 'teens when they were cowpokes on the
Chisum Trail. Over the Red River ol' Gene and him'd
go driving those lil' doggies up through Oklahoma
and Missouri where my grandpa taught ol' Gene to
hogtie and lasso and shoot straight with this gun my
grandpa still had in his holster in 1943 modern-day
San Francisco a real old pistol and Old Robert could
still shoot straight as he did at 22 and proved it the
next week when my father came around drunk to
woo back my mother mad at him, shot into the air
just 2 inches from my father's right ear. "Oh, honey,"
in 2002 says my Aunt Lil, Old Robert's last daughter,
"he was just pulling your little girl leg. Your granddaddy
never knew Gene Autry." Yes, he did. He knew ol'
Gene all right, I just saw him in that old cowboy movie
this morning on tv passing for Gabby Hayes shooting
straight at a city dude who looked just like my father
who'd have a ringing in his right ear until 1955.

ART LANGE

CLEAVE GREY

with yellow,
a slow,

spacious
light, Celtic

cairns, Cubist
cum laude,

vertical
opportunity,

a map, raw
image rubs

the blank
minutes.

Locates
a silk mirror,

floated
a purple web

turning
languorously

orange. Liquid
spilling each

petal, hands
spinning tone

island
still wet,

lathered with
praxis. In the

glowing
drawn a swipe,

all self-
imposed

portraits
pump trust

in chance,
chiming

elegies
to Cezanne,

lunar craters
and risk.

Static fields
inhabit

scarlet, glimpse
a Greek goddess'

thigh and
swerve.

Suffice
to cope with

the presence
of saints. Both

eyes

howl
in his head.

AFTERNOON

(after Tippett and Bunting)

Watching
these four strings

wrap around
your theme   a fleet

of birds verge home
crane cry   or tern

whisper   Neruda's violins
of chestnut

taut wound wires snap
and soothe

acres of brown grass and long
days empty

hours to rake blown leaves
dew wet

and dull
only ivy green or

fern leaf turned lace
by mist   a

twisted wrist to phrase
Corelli you quote

for solace
the faults beauty finds

late in life   breath shallow
too much moon

cold dissonant wind   song
all hearsay

KARIN RANDOLPH

ALL FUN & GAMES UNTIL

My brother mentions his scar again. I offer him an invisible Band-Aid &
separate the change, pennies in one bowl, silver in the other, like separating
darks into darks. Then I'm the one jumping on a bed again. I love to jump on
beds, my face, a small scurrying animal, not exactly afraid, but not bold.
Then knitting a baby-blue thing the exact color of a sky, never convinced the
thing will lift off, not exactly afraid.

Then flying to Chicago, stashing my booties under a seat, a thing which will
also float in emergencies. My brother who keeps mentioning the same thing. &
yes, I know the theory of air, less on top, more on the bottom, the stewardess
moving a pair of beautiful white hands like the gloves of a deaf woman.

Now someone else yelling knock it off or else. The air pressure under a wing,
my brother's head under a bed, a bed under the falling sky, but this is only a
theory, forgotten in the turbulence, I tell them I'm not deaf or dumb. The way
kids love Band-Aids & small furry animals & will often have them stuffed on
the beds they love to jump.

My mother who saves thick white sheets, who loves to watch the weather
channel. She says she wants to save everyone. I save Band-Aids just in case.
If I swallowed a fly or found a head under a bed. If a bed were found jumping
like a crazy kid with a small inside face. If my brother's stitches were only
quiet flies tickling his chinny chin chin. If my mother saved everyone with her
thick white sheets.

LIKE THE SLOW EATING OF RED MEAT

I slip on something a little more comfortable. Another went mad from the rain, sank as if in heavy snow. It must be snowing somewhere like dogs. In my version a cloud can weigh a ton, not to speak of gravity. First the cornice across the street that crumbled. Then the windshield smashed by kids. Then the man on Berry who jumped, some scattered rain. A large piece of rain that fell & hit, you could see its puddle with some blood evaporating to a damp spot.

It had teetered for years. I walk on the other side of the street just to be on the safe side. Just as I usually throw chain letters away at once, although I have not received one in years. Just as I eat meat like a pack of cards, like a small word you could easily slip between your teeth, like an umbrella or a lucky chain. I wonder if it will rain, if the puddle will dry in time, if the rain will be dry enough for once, the streets wet from a recent rain. How in the end no one could really say what he looked like. Someone said he resembled a cop so I imagine a cop in his uniform.

DAN SULLIVAN

CHRYSANTHEMUMS

fingertips
caught
in web
of last nights
spun by lock
stop
whether lips
made promises
if can't become
this nights.
he can't bury her
flowers—she
works
in a flower
shop.
they build
every thing
like walls
a moth savors
a panther's
presence

AMBER RESKEY

(As a wife hourly preserving four occasions)

UNABLE TO   **CIRCUMCISE**

Dear Lucy Snowflake,

Must you operate my chamber as man?
Forgive me when I forge my stay, as I am resting from your proposal.
Moreover, I have the knowledge of your carousel horse
Being occupied by a hairy mole.
She who would thrust forth your litter by the very name I surrender!
The rarity of a metal fence incasing your floor.
Love has curled up to die on such a floor!
Please, send me a peanut reason and I will race to your cottage.
We will discuss previous modes of sincerity.
I fear if you do not reply, I will continue in this vein for years.

Me

xoxoxoxoxoxoxoxoxoxoxoxoxoxoxoxoxoxoxoxoxoxox

Average men give us

Therapeutic publications

Swiftly, too!

I recommend

Carnage

shrewdness

suitable for one's own sake

In support of

Souvenirs

those explanations we half

eager for your velocity

Raven coals y knickers—Equivalent to milk bubbles—When they tuck fellow swayed—Since watt doctor shall receive such a notice—A splendidly dressed letter too pick up all her huff—the tawny gal laughs when the envelope is found intrusive and asked to shuffle back to a

, Our line of sexual calculation

Mother and I are presently discussing an antidote to delete these passages.

33

HAVE SITE

Sparrowing   boughs   of

a tired gallery.
          (Ex
                  Salt
      TINE)

Before such an inadequacy.

               Clean dishwater would have delighted your pacing feet,
                           callous as they were.

        Angle that which forsees
        disciples
        to flour.
        Crouched
inward
        Playing like dogs as dogs mating unsuccessfully.

        Eaves haunted these hands
        To longhorn of recite.

        After the apartment horror

        I reason,

                         day may be preferred.

Linked surrender?

since
we
have
no
little
ones
rum
stitches
our
complexities
with
her
rubber
thumb

Vowels of censure
Make eager
Low tunes.

~~Over here for torsoing~~

We need an architect!

Or a little man.

Welcome to division of rent with sudden muted tangos.

But I turn to confronting
knuckles—

Rousing, no more.

JEFFERY CONWAY

EIGHTEEN

Although I was drunk,
I saw her apartment had
a homey décor.

This made it easy
to relax when our party
came ashore on her bed.

She preached against TV,
wore huge triangle earnings,
vied to be crowned queen

of my virginity.
Her black skirt caught the wind
of the window fan

revealing the icon
of chiefs and gods,
soft volcanic tuff.

I landed, mottling
the sheets, a jet airplane on
the tarmac's gold line.

In antiquity's
workshop, I was a big flop.
Next day, the others

found my skeleton
among the boxes, reeds and
grasses. Red canoes,

voyaging across the
Pacific, loaded down with
blood oranges, shoes,

came to my rescue:
boys extended brotherly
affection. The end.

I WANT TO BE—

most days I can't remember,
and at moments dead,
but as of late
I'd like to be the expressive hand
and give you all the dirt.

I want to be unashamed,
the teller of all things,
like, for example, the writer
of letters answering your questions
about my sex life:

I can't explain "the boot in the face,"
but if I were there, or you here
I'd sit for hours or days—
as long as it takes—

and you'd understand
that mostly I want to be Opie:
he takes Pa's advice and learns
to laugh when he's punched
in the eye by that darn bully
who waits each day
to dole out the pain
on my bright happy way home.

I want to be unconscious,
not knowing that what lies
ahead is really more of the same.

I want to be touched,
and when I wake,
I am swimming naked just off shore—

it's the last perfect moment I know—
I'm bobbing like a buoy
in semi-wavy water

where the sun slaps down from the sky,
a day so perfect
I eat two pieces of Aunt Bee's pie.

DANIEL NESTER

FROM *GOD SAVE MY QUEEN*

FLASH'S THEME

This description of Earth from afar, yes, by Death Itself.[72] I picture the silent screening, the four of them, again with wonderful jackets. A large Italian man heaves up rumors in that first conversation.

Sixteenth note in a decade destined to go down the tubes, and voices intermingling still, then silence. "Nice bass line," the cashier from the local record store said, fingering his suburban punk mullet. I stood there like a pussy.

Camp Wagner has begun.

---

72 Max Von Sydow, The Emperor Ming, aka "Ming the Merciless"; *The Seventh Seal* (Igmar Bergman, 1957).

FOOTBALL FIGHT

We could have been in a porno, Dark Brothers-style; we could have plunked ourselves in the booth, just the four of us, the five of us, and it would have been the best music ever for a stag film. Ever.

Instead, we stuck in this mimesis of sex, a shadowgame of onomatopoeia, wrestling money shots, bottoms-up. We can only do this for a few seconds before petering out, mistaken for dutiful loop-de-loops.

Disappointment at end, dry-faced, glass-crashed.[74]

---

74 *New Wave Hookers* (1985).

EXECUTION OF FLASH/ THE KISS
(AURA RESURRECTS FLASH)

Slid down a triad, a feeling, a husk, an actual empathetic moment—a voice in the end, a voice in the uppers. Someone must die. The voices know that. We feel sadder than we're supposed to. And this confirmation lies where?

Only in the regnal passageway of our voices, where there can be no rehearsal.

SHARON DARROW

MILTON

Lost:

1.

> *(darkness visible)*
>
> forbidden
> mortal taste
>
> restore the blissful
> secret chaos
>
> I thence invoke
> dove-like
>
> abyss favored
> guile of rebel angels
>
> in glory opposed
> headlong flaming

2.

> *(defy his horrid crew)*
>
> as far
> as from
>
> unlike
> with floods
>
> silence
> yet not
>
> nor what
> do I repent
>
> fierce
> innumerable
>
> plains
> of heaven

3.

(apostate angel)

to suffer suffice
do service
avail or eternal

speedy Cherub
whom we seek
to pervert

& disturb
in storm surge
the precipice

falling
thunder red
& impetuous

vast & boundless
you dreary light
livid pale & dreadful

4.
(in hue subterranean)

there rest if rest resembling offend calamity blaze a rood consult
Leviathan haply fixed under the lee reiterated himself Evil enraged

5.

(concerning fire)

torn or shattered Etna

thus low

extinct & happy
dusky weight

seduced
in endless

guile   shame

in billows on each hand

upheld defeat

as gods

lost

6

(thou hell)

solid liquid fire

thy new possessor

be free

in my choice

faithfull

Beelzebub

on the perilous edge

on yon lake

amazed

large & round

the moon

7.

(foresight by fate)

optic   artist   spotty
burning   marl   smote
his   legions   autumnal
where   vexed   waves
beheld   perfidious
sojourners   carcasses
broken   wheels   lay
under   hideous   change

PAULA KONEAZNY

FROM *SENTENCE*

(November 4-10, 2001)

Uncertainty particularizes the next sentence—not trying to go anywhere or meet anyone. His adroit avoidance of risk, coupled with his passion for imagined geography, brings you (or to be truthful, some version of you) to mind. Lost in the hotel, the boy and I are accomplices now, as are our counterpart personal items (my white racing stripes and his neon signs). When she severs the past from the future, she hears him say from the other side, "I'm allergic to violence." There are storage compartments beneath vowels—Ramallah—like silk evening gowns (I see only his feet). Where does the hand puppet fit in? Pegasus appears to her not as the winged horse wearing the golden bridle but as a fracture running through the material.

TOM JOHNSON

STEALTHY PEOPLE NEED TUTELAGE

This could be co evil. Alls they wished,
afters all, was a distant cousin coming
bearing pennies. And their stalks were
not too tall, possibly in defense. Is that
not too good? It's too good. The lots
were separated * chairs tables T.V.s
books. The whole lot of them in die
verge. Bad company. Kind of putrid.
Kind of

       Certain foots raw
           unproportioned little have nots
           convulsing from the freezer,
           palmed disorder
                  because no one gleamed
                  and no one shared feelings

It was not salvageable
      and
It was not sacred
      to
plume the patriarch
when rage met the
weather.

Really, their magnets were opposites
attracting only broth—particle vile.

So distant cousins stayed distant.

In descent, number one number two number three number four number five
    number six etc.
           frolicked in a whirlpool
           of minerals
           strobing an earthquake

And so this presents introductions

but lazarous moods (lastly)
jeered
        the newsPAPERS
because flashing
        exempts
bundles of shrill
        knuckles.

As was documented
        on a
clay cave wall.

BARON WORMSER

WHEN BILLY MOVED BACK HOME

I think it was around 1979 and his fifth group—
    Tragic Package—
That he saw the graffiti on the bathroom wall,
    Not literally
(Though there was that too) but existentially,
    Which is to say,
Sober. "Morning is bad for people," he said
    More than once and
He wasn't posing. That clean, early sunlight
    Startled him, turned
His hazy stomach over. "I've lived the rock life,"
    He'd mutter—meaning
Two near-electrocutions, twenty-some guitars, enough
    Fast food to choke
An elephant, small debts from here to Seattle,
    Strands of women's hair,
Sore throats . . . but what did counting ever do
    Except please the accountants?
He was never going to be more than an opener, good
    But a lot less than great.
He wondered what his feelings would do without that playing,
    How would his soul thrive
The way it did when he got down and wailed?
    He'd wilt, he would
Be another busy civilian. Ecstasy had possessed him on
    Numerous occasions; he
Had shivered with violent joy and given it to others.
    That must be what morning
Was for, that forgiving light, the people all tidy
    And going off to work.
He'd answer the phone, shop, go to the dentist.
    And when he practiced
It would be for the sake of it, the notes that went
    Nowhere and loved it.

CLASS OF '65 (1990)

"The lights are going out already," my mother says
In reference to some of my classmates from
    Sturtevant High School who
Though they would have been only in their forties
    Are gone:

The casualties of AIDS, heart attacks, car crashes,
And the common cancers that are the unyielding ghosts
    In the polymer paradise.
I nod in agreement although I'm in another room
    Eating

Slices of American cheese and pimiento loaf
And staring at an article about a movie star
    Who drowned in his Saturnalia-
Sized swimming pool. I reflect that you don't see
    Mortality's

Face much in the glossies where life looks like one
Long languorous orgasm of cleavage, jeans and vodka.
    Nor do you see the Dance of Death
Strutting its leering stuff in the malls and outlet stores,
    Banging

Bones on hubcaps and metal trashcan covers
And keening the contralto funk of time.
    My mother, meanwhile, goes back
To the crossword puzzle in the *TV Guide* and then
    To the tube

Where even when people are trying to be rational
They're yelling. They're always a couple of decibels
    Above polite conversation, to say
Nothing of the intimate whispers that are the dearest
    Tokens

Of our permeable humanity. My mother leaves me thinking
About Chuck Meola and Binky Smith and Iris Prendergast.
    For some immeasurable seconds
Their pure adolescent incandescence vibrates
    Like one

Of those back-of-the-classroom raspberries startling
The reverie of a droning afternoon. In the other room,
    The television chortles and brays.
My vision vanishes; the lights go out amid relentless
    Laughter.

SHANA CLEVELAND

THE DISTANT THUNDER ROAR

at some point i lost my boy. i looked around
the beach where the sky was always almost
storming & the air was cool and humid as
breath. i wanted to call him, but when i
found his number there were others there
too, all hard to make out. i tried
calling one. a woman answered. she was
white and her house always smelled like
food. she sat in her food house with her
daughter and they were having a good laugh
over my mistake. FUCK YOU, i yelled,
FUCK YOU FUCK YOU & buried the
receiver.

i went to his mother's house, which was
very dark. she had dogs who seemed to
multiply as we sat there. she was dark in
every conceivable way. she seemed to like
me, but soon there would be far too many
dogs.

THE DOG DAYS

it was rainy, but not so much that it made us
wet. i was in love with you in a demeaning
scenario. you did not love me. you acted
like a little boy in your velvet jackets and
billowing white shirts. in your pointed
boots. a willowy little boy. it's so nice, you
said, the coming without the going.

then my plane would crash. I jump out
and run as the air allows, which is something
like a dramatic stroll. there are other people
running. their expressions range between
terror and mild concern.

LAKE PLACID

we stood, the three of us, in the hallway for a
good long while. they were changing but
pretty. there was a lewd understanding,
which we spoke around, grinning like
villains. my cosmopolitan was beading,
leaking in my hand, but i was so.

Susan came up with golden pigtails that
held the light like a sling, & ice skates over
one shoulder. she talked like we were
listening. when she finally turned to go we
stole a few strands, thinking they might be
worth something.

we got the news around dusk, casting a
morbid shadow over our night plans. when
they pulled her from the water her hair was
dark like mine. a dozen geese stood stoic.
i regretted that cosmopolitan remark.

TIM DONAHOE

KLEENEX

how profound

life is when

your arm is caught

in a meat grinder

I never ate

panda is that so

wrong every time

I hung a picture

I was aiming for

my fingers and

I always hit the

nail on the head

perfectly hung

the picture and

walked away

feeling like a

failure is that

perverse like

sex in a port

o potty some

one told me

when I was

down one

day that beauty was

all around me all

I needed to do

was open my eyes

but I'm no insomniac

because of beauty

to me beauty is like

a fresh wad of cum

sometimes you

need to jack

off to see it

but seriously I

would love to

eat an endangered

species burger just

once and I wish my

eyes weren't closed

every time something

of beauty was made

but I guess beauty

is a lot like a

sneeze, messy.

FOLDER

The Braille cliff of a brow; a flare in the hot beast

grunts below planks. A fluttered line,

saving them all later;

dice that roll slowly

over and lose sense.

Fell in the oven trying

to relieve the anguish of stuffing.

Winning is as it is pushed

towards a seven or a corner as lint shaved

from fingernails in your very own pocket.

Last dream involved none of the following:

*before I felt myself falling

*cobras at the fifth station

*hair rain

Message on hand left imploded

noted and forgotten just as

times that don't fade

they are consumed in the soon after

flash of gold in your pocket.

The dream that I will have tonight is definitely hard to grab a hold of.
A pinch.

Even tear; examine will

kill. The small pet of the shadow

nothing but the wash can remove

the glint of flame beneath the press

and the steady immersion, the suds,

the gasping.

EVONNE ACEVEDO

CRUISING THE FISH

We have also what are called monstrosities, but they graduate into varieties. —Darwin, *Origin Of Species*

Consider love occurring in vague quantity
and you hasten the ceremony,
preserve that false suitable operation
for your nobler darling, that
vocal torso made excellent by the
fallacy in his bones, his glistening
asphyxiation and the sex that heaved
louder; you kiss the livid hand,
the wrenched mouth, trail staggering
for days the body, wail at
the moon waxed fingers
dripping into the eddies—

Consider invalids in volume,
twisted at the marrow, flat
orange eyes favoring candy, useless.
Novelty and loss immediate as
blossoms, to be ladled and flung—
sore benign beauties not demanding
love. Somehow it is embarrassing,
the obtusity of mourning—
the customers are coming and
have no taste
for the literal, oblong dead.

BILL KUSHNER

FLAMING CREATURES

Saturday, another dragon goes by, such
flaming creatures, I forgive my life. Master
goes by, wave waves, we are made of lovers
a mangy dog sniffs a fearful leaf, lifts leg
& pees, looks back in remembrance, one
furry blink, then growls him on. What are
we saved from, what will survive us, in
a pinch, a storm? A step in the park, a
statue stumbles & falls to a heap, a bird
squawks up. Those who see visions walk
our streets in a scream, we'd best avoid them
for they tell us nothing we don't already
know, we were all born in mangers, let
us go forth, come. Kid dances on a corner
& all for our nickels, as we gather round him
all we heroes & villains, all we lost, we found.

10/26/02

ZERO STAR MOTEL

for Anselm Berrigan

Call me Mister Poisonality. Ishmael
says me & Stevie we saving up to buy
the Playboy Mansion. Yeah, goofballs
rain. Sometimes, like everyone else,
wonder why do I bother to awake every
morning, say around noon, to dash my
self nude red upon those cold rocks I
call my bed, & then to face that mirror
with its startling reflection: are you really
me? Time oh time you skid on by, &
leaving all these marks, oh well well, go
Saints. A strange foot becomes a stranger
just leaving, Pal, tanks. Outside, they
line up to get inside, where pleasure a-
waits, & the girls dance slowly, ever so
slowly, as if time meant nothing, & such
faraway looks on their dreamy faces, so
one wants to ask them what visions are
you seeing? all the young men are won-
dering, but too shy to stand up, as if
they could. O just to emerge way away
past midnight, caught in pools of limpid
moonlight, there to stand & shimmer,
if for just a moment, & then for home.

10/27/02

THURSTON MOORE

INVISIBLE STORY

fantastic and calm
and fantastic and sure of violence
david rattray
is dead.
in his notebook
a page is adorned w/ question marks.
significant i.d.s
into thoughts of music
(in nomine)
music
essentially ends
the book
drifts out
in doubled dream.

death rips these pages a flipped out bride
dull journals of american poets blowing weed
in love w/ each other's eloquence
in beat madness
in episodes of brotherhood
death conspires to reveal a sad smile,
& surprisingly so.

surrealism has come to america
to unify you angels
& to alert you
to uniformed fuzz.

& surrealism—
stowaway information
(artauds escapade, crevels sensual eye)
gives david rattray
a charge of true love
& the translators translation of death:
come home to me,
dear god.

REBECCA BRIDGE

THE LAST TIME NICK SAN ANTONIO WENT FISHING

for Cody San Antonio

The wind's breath came labored and ragged,
smelled of the browning grasses he had spent
weeks romancing (softly kissing in all the
right places) and only just then had he gotten these
rustling ladies to lay themselves down for him.

The cattails stood in mourning, leaned across the
banks of a river, bodies held rigid as bones,
threw the fluff of their heads to the river
(like offerings of flowers), stood silently
watching as some things floated away.

The river that once rolled boulders
lazily resigned itself to plinking pebbles along
(and only this occasionally)
while clerical minnows swam crosses and blessings
beneath the currents of its waters then made holy
(And was this why the cicadas had been crying?)

An old split-wood dock ran an aisle out
into the river against which a tied-up blue canoe beat
and thumped ever-slowing rhythms.
A plastic bag hung from a gnarled log post,
was a lung filling up with wind
(emptying itself of wind),
and a rusted coffee can laid on its side
while dirt and such things spilled out.

The weeping willow cast its branches out
towards the river, reeled them in, cast again,
baited leaves squirming in the breeze
(a fisherman patient for the big one).
The boy laid in its shadows,
made o's of his mouth, held a hand against
his chest and the willow dropped a leaf
beside him.

THE FAT DRIPPINGS OF A WAS-BEAUTIFUL AFTERNOON

for Mom

It was a beautiful afternoon. Dog pee
glistened and dripped from the daffodil's firm
petals. An alley cat had run the length
of a chain link fence, paused, then vanished
beneath the screened-in porch. There
he devoured his bird and make-believe bacon.

"There are some children who believe bacon
grows on trees!" called my mother in her tulip-y
voice. (You see, this was just before the doctor took from there
in her belly a piece of liver, charcoaled and firm,
said "As we suspected, cancer!" and then winked and vanished
to lunch on ham sandwiches, going on at length

about the number and individual names and lengths
of the boats in his toy fishing fleet to the bacon-
skinned janitor from El Salvador.) But cancer vanishes
at certain decibels of memory. From the sidewalk came, "I won't eat peas!"
All the children were running, shrieking, and, though the mothers were firm,
we could still hear the sounds of plates breaking. Oh, and remember how
    their

fathers came hastily from the corner pub where their
pool game had been interrupted and laughed heartily at the lengths
their wives would go to be free of dishes? You held me firmly,
asked me back to the bedroom . . . but enough! We had been talking of
    bacon
and finding mothers with rashers of it growing in their organs and weren't
    we happy?
Please, we thought, do let's speak quickly before the afternoon vanishes!

Not that an afternoon could ever really vanish.
Really what an afternoon does is like, well, there's
an old wives' tale, right? Never mind that, we just peed
in the bushes, after all, the afternoon was not terribly lengthy,
and old wives didn't get to cook bacon
(or eat it either) unless they first killed the pig. I said, "Firmly,

tell me have you ever felt your feet much upon the firmament?
Well, maybe you did in those moments that always seemed to vanish

just when you realized that you'd bought a pig's worth of bacon
to feed a house of vegetarians. And there, there
shh, I know, sugar, it's like trying to stay clean, how you go to such lengths
and wash your hands, but then every time you shower, you pee."

And then you sighed, "I suppose bacon *is* luckier than beef. There's
nothing so firm and yet tender as the sun before it vanishes
hissing into the evening, like a length of snow that melts under cat pee."

ANDREW EARLY

PHOTOGRAPHIC MOMENT

Photographic moment: a time
captured by memory—a small
pair of boys shoes knotted
and thrown over power line from
my house to alley pole.

Tower on top of building adjacent
(I still don't know what it's for)
they're all over the city,
this one blocks the sun.

Old, old Chicago brick encloses,
a construction worker next door
just took a piss in the wide
open, stopped not when he saw me
but when his bladder was emptied
of the Big Gulp variety.

Bzzzzzzzzzzzzzat, bzzzat! Buzz
saws intermittently while
shoes dangle precariously.

Trash heap obscured by
slotted chain link (the fence
also keeps out torsos) and
Gregory Corso.

JEANNE MARIE BEAUMONT

GOOD MORNING

Here at our channel, we do it now so we can chat about it later. Verbs are moguls to us. Ours is a precinct of urgency and tenderness.

Go ahead, open the curtains, silly. It's no longer Tuesday, but the signs are still up. Are you afraid of being seen? It's not what it used to be. The compacter is running, the disposal is running. You'll have to talk a bit louder, using more common words and assuming a provocative tone.

We're receiving isolated reports of leftovers burning in the northern suburbs. Stubborn particles still remain.

Think of *Vapor-Action!* as a pick-me-up. We call that progress.

Now, bow to the household gods of spin, screen, drone, and slam. Perch on the handiest newel post and repeat after me:

The rain falls first on the radar and then in our mouths.

Oh, you're good.

FROM THE ANNALS OF PERSEVERANCE

Bent over overlapping *O*'s of the copybook

         Between Cleanliness and Self-control (—traits)

. . . *in spite of failure*

              "picked yourself up brushed yourself

Oaf shook the table, spilling/

         spoiling the meniscus; she rose

    to fetch the pitcher and filled the glass again.

  Unquiet nights in steerage

  unquiet stagecoach

        Proceeded down a long aisle:

    managing the crutches managing

to crack the code not breaking the code not then

        Rewards of the method drone.

Slogging through   (much later?)

          . . . *in spite of* fright *really*

    submitting over & over & over

  Drip, it drips, has dripped, will keep dripping,

      Tying knots with frozen fingers

>Bitter End<

      Penning the linked O's better!

In which the child   earned an A*

CHRISTOPHER NERI

TITLES FOR POEMS THAT DON'T EXIST

Falling Apart Over the Laundry

One Winter That Never Happened

Make Me My Morning

Wedding Dress Stains and Regrets

Things I've Stepped On

10 Pennies Worth of Twenty Watt Light

Birdshit

Everyday the Mailman Comes

The Fingernail Canoe

The Whiskey Lamp at The End of The Alley

Steel Frame Monsters

Tumble

Life For a Sock

You're Only Saying That Because I Have a Gun

KYLEE COFFMAN

IT'S LIKE THIS

They are coming for me; I know it. Like dogs for a bone,
like the tick of clock.
My foot, naked and waiting, moisturized, manicured toenails,
ready for that crystal pump.
He's coming.
It's like this;
I wait around, say fifty years and sing a lot, in case the birds
are spies.
Sure there is laundry and spider webs,
but it's just practice
for the palace,
in case the maid ever gets in a jam.
You'll see.
They are coming for me.
My bag is packed. I listen to "These boots are made for walkin'"
fifty times, on repeat.
It's a curse, really.
And they *all* know it. My family, the neighbors. I send them letters
telling them how much I'll miss them when I'm in the big house.
I make a list of destination honeymoons:
Cancun, Niagra Falls, Istanbul.
I make lists of what I should pack:
toothbrush, robe, sunglasses, plenty of underwear.
I read up on sex tips
for the prince and all.
You know, nobody is a Puritan *these* days and the prince
really deserves the best a girl can give him.
So I sing my songs,
let my hair grow and stare at the drive
for any suspicious looking limos or carriages.
My bag is packed by the front door half open
like an exit sign,
a little green case,
ready for a quick escape.

PERSONAL POEM

Hiss

Everybody on the train looks like they're hiding something,
even the old lady with her cane.
The suit, the tourist, even me with my little notebook. Even I
just want to read aloud like the slip of someone with really
tight headphones.
I have sympathy for the elderly. I think the elderly should never
have to ride the train, cut their toenails, or put out their cigarettes.
Elderly People Should Smoke! would be my campaign
if I ever ran for President.
But I can't run today, my knees are sore.

What's in the bag, old bag?
    My nausea. Ouch! My pain, my pain.

The train stops. I get off.
My knees are kicked in and bruised
from last night's show. Too much whiskey, after all, it's free!
TV says it's Wednesday, better move. I moved once
and then again and then again. I'm always moving.
A lady asks me what street it is. I tell her, but wish I'd lied.
I see a penny, but it's face down.

    There are ads for health bars and people who laugh too loudly.
Shh! My head aches. Laugh quietly, please.
Instead of eating a health bar, I made a sandwich.
I hate breakfast foods. Why are they always so sweet?
If I was president I'd outlaw breakfast. Kids would wake up to
sandwiches and cigarettes. But it's Wednesday, gotta work.
gotta learn gotta grow-up gotta brush my hair
        gotta take two asprin gotta swallow Don't choke! gotta
call mom and dad and sis and Jeff and it's Rachel's birthday!
        gotta be on time gotta turn everything in on time gotta move
gotta look both ways gotta feed the goldfish just enough so his water
        doesn't turn green.

TOM CLARK

DRIFTING

A trumpet vine
a bright green
tree fern—the
violet light
of early evening
fog enshrouds
pink big
city clouds

HERBERT KROHN

MY GEORGIA ISLAND TREEHOUSE

Peeing from my treehouse at night. It spreads out and strikes palmettos with a monsoon clatter. A flashlight illuminates the peefall standing in space. Sometimes I finish before the pee has reached earth. Then, like me, it's on its own in life.

National Geographic says in the Amazon there are little swift fish that can swim upstream with barbed heads to lodge in a penis. I could turn it off and on in Morse code to baffle them.

I'm not afraid of them here in the treehouse. I'm not afraid of rolling out while I sleep, though in the city I'm afraid the floor will lower and I'll wake in a bed on a pylon. And in the city I'm always afraid that a hand or foot left over the edge of the bed will be stripped by the carnivorous dustfish of my bedroom.

JONATHAN MINTON

"THERE IS NO JAZZ IN THE SOUTH," HE SAID.

Thus discovering is

> the expectation
> of proper taste: such eloquence as

>> tucked straw tuft, clipped
>> drawl, civilizing
>> dredge
>> of raw coal

>> (innocent ears
> hear nothing

> (thus said
> (of is, & said as

>> —*Crow Feather*, dark as
>> —*Coal Dust*, scattered as
>> —*Moth-*
>>> *wing.*
>> as motes   clinging
>>> there at a point, there
>>> to a point, and there
>> (in throat
>>> "as is"—broken or not

> *kittlebottom: is coal lump big as a tub*

>> (of which the copula is a partial local
>> translation: Louis is here, Louis
>> is there: this is partially local, therefore

>> in the idiom of either

>> this is how one speaks   (of false mem-
>>> branes, remembering

>> *ai*, or *ay*, signals
>>> in a mineshaft assemblage:

thus discovering

>> ....
>> is airborne
>> is lungful of dust

71

DEMETRIA JONES

THE POCKET-WATCH PROMISE

In a five-framed snapshot tucked within the casing of my windowsill, the girl disintegrates. The false connection from the plastic phone, the white piglet snorting away the silent-eye glint, my father no longer exists—his tailored suit royal to the cause, my king. Black velvet hat tipped, tight-mouth smile—this photo comprises the promise. This tick-tick-ticking nuisance hemmed to the pleats of my red polka-dot dress. I am queen with my counterfeit bunch of flowers—make me the pretty girl. Hand in hand, the prettied puppets make belief of happy. We are swallowed within the frame . . . the intensity of focus, camera-snap, bury the real for tragic.

LOVE NOT

Because I didn't think you would mind,
and we were lovers for a spell.
The casting on and off,
this life was much simpler.
Our conversations trailing out the backdoor,
and no one would ever know.
Yesterday was the last time we . . .
I recall the blue of your shadow
within the glare of the television set
while Audrey Hepburn gave us pointers.
Did we talk about that?
I mentioned old loves to a friend.
Your name never came up.
I found your number folded in my mattresses,
between the new guy and the older sheets.
Trailing out the back door,
conversations muffled within
unknowing stares of someone
we both might have known.
I didn't think you would mind so . . .

ARMAND F. CAPANNA II

THE LITTLE FISH OF SUBLIME GRACE

But,   a sequence   of judgments found,

  Lacking to manifest, a solitary ballet   beyond

Geography,   own   synchronology   . . . (what speaks:
    Methods of fertility floun-
                ders in what laws do they obey?)

                "*Their features make me ill . . .*"

Mobile breach

Des- troyed in

Br-   *y*

(each) so   young that bound

Up/ever   In objects absolved *not merely* myths, in fact,

        Singe he speaks: should simple relegate

        A term/alone used an abused apostrophe

        Fall up/on a much accidental in,

        Speech is thrown or delved by bastards par-

        Old propoise "she got hand" chived in

        Rhymed I wept."

Cordage to "no . . . *this* phrase" respirates effused in dorsal box(ed) cower,
    chewed he did, flesh of personal odor
        In order,   to elude the crotch of informal influence(za)

        That t'   urns man

        In grace with

        Fingers watching seeds

        That gnaw.

FROM CRUMPETS

If this is written, I am not the one. —Arkadii Dragomoschenko

But, of any lives............

............are failures, in some trumpeted form, marches another letter
reconstructing   grammar indistinct.   The real havoc   is frozen ground not
traveled from the region in   *this* region, one can no longer see the banners flown
                                      against the incinerated city.

          What do these words matter? Grain for the snowstorm? A compliance   the narrative is slick
a greedy body, ambiguous like September? On the finished slopes,
with secrets immersed in an ample sea's dream.   Which after the head has been thrown back, a mutiny conducted,
          what laws apply? How does one open the curtain, the voyeur and a peep show cracked open   in the bandage of the
word's derailed train, I   yield with a throat of glass, a cavity,   category at the end of rotation

§

Now, as if the ice, lasting by   another face, a war recall, undoubtedly heart
          of the story arrived with the morning roars of a drowned era. And on the walls. stalactite sprig
                    crumpled by the weight of a Spring, shape   of a vowel lost in the
          margin's porous nothing. the   *sound* of nothing and   the death of my neighbors

§

Root as if. harbored the vain, the bullfighter, ceasing a flow like a windmill.   Matched the primordial   offerings.
          O' you as in *not precious*, this draft, a
                    dumbness of author. Certainly.   Firm in the pasty torpor, reducing
the face to a name   in fact, hardly an obstacle to decline further respiration   A migration.
The city sockets   is a prospect in pocket size

75

Death by no feigns hero plot of density, itself a clay grain, a crow cracks in a howl barrier   the sky.   The past - ellipse. The event. *Is* an event split in directions. a liberty of words? Probably soon arctic cadaver, nailed   the form of familiarities, cancels this by the bush of the sun. Scorch no longer something in   final goodbye.   Tell it to the sea, the beast you see, a parallel of snow.

Multiplying itself beyond a tired sum of plot. the vision turns
to the texture of coal, but of the text bone hisses
with the perfection of an earned frost, a vacant land   populating from the mouth
A generation of families, of relations huddling in the crook of the flame. And winter ash

Of years.

§

The sour-filled ache, and the old man is adamant on pension. he gums. and the cinder fumes from the marks of ancient times, I, chopping with war, thunder by the worm's home. Grid of history. Map maker drunk on the widows kind misery   *simple* slip of marionette cocoons the dead who search for mercy on the banks of the Seine.

§

And each shall erase a person. The pedestrian standing outside, the eyes echo and snow in the man's shoe, bog of the terrain. Your face, has not scene before. And in death's canopy, we'll
sleeve through miles on foot. All this
meaning, nothing held for the great river, a conversation, and as before, the   same
absurdness of a gravity at the end with the **Ends.**

§

Smoke after, the scrapping of the white   boils down to haze
in the eyes burn, the unbearable labyrinth of a splashed reading. However . . . frequently by laughter,
by death and   the material of the dark in the Seine, squelched by speech, the ruminating victims and Celan,
all the while plays the fool among   winter, and the hours he spends enmesh
mouth and utters *gawd, whatever* into dumbness they   are the core, the point at which
I needle and cut stones in my jaw tenderly, stand by water itself chilled
by the rotted flesh.

§

Anyways. we do   not depart all to   gather the effects of the coming storm.   In the tune
of night's trap a, coming of utterance, pressing the ear into the floor   board, precious
acts of solitude. *The sequence of things changed rarely.* On the side aches. Tomorrow. I'll
go home, wash my body beside the ravine, and later, gorge
on flower paw of language.

§

Without having to end, the   figure is spilled in a concept, the ovary of a text, only
to yield again: the hoarfrost.

§

77

CHARLES BERNSTEIN

FIVE FOR M.P.

Maybe
approaching—
ridges,
journeys—
overtakes
rips
in
eternity.
Please
encase
rough
loaves
on
festive
flames.

Myriad
acrobatic
rusts
jar
overlays,
rile
intermittent
envelopes.
Play
everything,
rush
lunges,
occasion
forging
formulation.

Myrrh
and
roses
jar
ovation,
running

into
elemental.
Pack
enough
ropes
lest
overflow
faults
fate.

My
answer
revolves—
jerkily!—
on
radiant
interior
expression.
Polkadot
encaustic
ripples,
lilts
of
foraging
figments.

Maybe
anyway
radiant
jumble
or
really
incomparable
evanescence.
Particular
encounters
revealing
lingering
oases,
festooned
flutes.

NICHOLAS RAVNIKAR

LOGOCIDE AND PATROLOGISMS

Every time you make love you tamper with fate. —Michael Blumenthal

      filth   in   the blink

      Disenclosure payday?

I ran like I ran that night (in mind)   and your face like a sweat-frothy beast

Image: lengths of steel cable coming forth with precious spittle from your pale mouth.

Oh. Fax. When is a poem
always a poem? When it's
inging its ethics, "obliterating..
...................................self-consciousness"

of its characters:: liminal riff-raph(ael's

                      contraceptive means of anonymity

                      prophylactic buttons of a gruff phallocentrist

                      aptitude for impulsion—compulsion

                      registered, thinged, inging-ing

                      graphite carries armature to I am hungry

                       but not to

                      I am eating

Poesis of created is the

(f)act of halation and

perspiring (pulmonary and

respiratory, in addition to

nervous activity)—dripping

the beads hung
on the forehead—lapsed
elliptically to the poem
Object and reader
Subject through   /you's/
of pneumonic poesis, for
"Poems [themselves] do not necessarily make the beholder
conscious of his or her role . . . nor can such self
-consciousness be obliterated only by presenting
highly visualizable scenes . . . " (quote, Charles Bernstein)

      reality,

      as such

      is the best

      "poem"

      Yet

      poems

      the best

      "reality"

      ever, co

      or(di)nate

      -ly.

[4: LOVE POEM]

I eat

peanut

Butter

and straw

berry jam,

re-

member your name

a thing-full

of beauty.

Your

face cannot

recall completely.

A tooth

places

here or there. *out*.

Your eyes. I am

shut.

Negating. But

I cannot see

thee

at this time, so

your name is

all I have

to think on.

RYAN PHILIP KULEFSKY

I AM THE PIONEER OF THE DANCE FLOOR

after Creeley

Dear bird—
you are

smarter than
I though,

lacking a
proper girth

which gives
you charm,

we eat
you for

breakfast and
like it.

> June 30th, 2002
> 2:41 p.m.

BAN THE BUMS: AN ALEATORICAL SONNET

He babbled through his caked on
bowels and swore on his censured

goldenrodded Biblical brooks, the.
Even today it's a notorious new

Sunday of the outran hullabaloo clam
bake evenings before. Knobby poems'

lustra bare the last brunt of take
as we fright too, but progress, dainty

with insouciant gallivant eating
the sweet exotics of our own crap.

The lingering evermore of stink
phagocytes: tail fuzzy brown classic

undergarments and bend out toldings
the shape of orange cream steel boors.

March 7, 2001

KAREN NEUBERG

YOLKS

Mama was as cruel as ever. In her starched white apron, she appeared at our door and brought the traditional newlywed cake. Except she failed to fill it with charms that would bring us good fortune. All I found was a button that belonged to a smock my dead sister had owned. I cried when I saw what it was. Mama smiled.

Not that it ended there. I was supposed to be the daughter who replaced my sister. My sister died as a consequence of an act of her own will. She had stepped off the edge of the cliff beside our house. Mama and papa were arguing and chanced to turn just in time to see her go over. They arrived at the rim in time to see her skirts caught in a billow as she floated out and down. My sister waved to them and continued her descent. She landed safely on both feet but slipped off the rock as she looked up at them to stick out her tongue. She drowned in two feet of water because she could not swim and did not think to stand up. Lack of a mere detail or I would have an older sister and none of this would be mine.

A few months after I was married, I felt restless and went to mama for advice. She told me that what I needed was a baby. Or a new hat. Soon it would be the Day of the Parade and everyone would stroll down the Avenue of Bygones in memory of the past year. One had to have at least a new hat or a new baby. Mama secured the boiled yolks of a dozen eggs onto a silver plate and told me it was my hat. My husband garnished it with parsley and ashes. I was photographed many times that Parade Day. The pictures appeared in newspapers and magazines around the world. We made up a name for each yolk and told everyone that it stood for the name of a child I would someday have. Little golden faces looking up to the sun. The silver plate's brim cast a shadow over my eyes so that they were hidden. Had I been able to see them in the pictures, I would have known I was carrying our first child, her temperament caught in flecks of light in my iris. I was busy being a celebrity. My husband was unusually solicitous. Mama was smiling unusually wide. Why not, she had already won. Inside one of the yolks swam a strand of my sister's hair.

JASON NOAH

DEITY

they all get
to fuck you
and wash clean feet

afterwards
i invite them
for wines and chants

that is just
the sort of antagonist
i vowed to be

equipped
with the gospels
to prove i am

mistaking nothing for nothing
for i am not
an intellectual

constructing you a face
to ignore your soul
as if you are simple

and i am hungry
enough to consume
the metaphors

ATTENTION

where there was only air,
cluster, and impeccable shape, i drew
lines leading to the next lines;
the picasso tip is what i christened
my fruitful finger, but knew no picasso
(liked the foreignish piece of letters
<sounded pick asshole, but would never say so
dreading old hand soap and getting
lodged in a dirty word drain for leaving
the house naked>)and only wanted to draw
a language to make visits and ineptly
transmit   (i got stared at a lot)

LINDA OH

POINTS

The plums are orange.
Crisp.

Peel a pea. Lose the vine. Loose the pollen.
Let us pray. Around the apples. Apples are to eat.
Tart.
Apples are to eat.

Praises are silent.
Pomegranates lay in silence
in palms and these palms press
in motion
leaving the
apples lying
under the garbage
inviting the mice
to feast in silence.

DRINKING, GIRLS, ETC.

It's two days to Halloween.
I've associated this holiday with hellish hours at work—
yuppies frantic in their search for the perfect nurse outfit
or paisley '70's shirt that everyone else will wear too.
I am not thinking about dressing up—I don't do that.
Just like I don't dance either.

When it was 5 days to Halloween
I checked bags for eight hours and got a $22 bonus
I promptly spent on Stella, the beer.
I didn't eat much that day and got drunk fast.
I walked around in the cold, rosy-cheeked,
pushing my bike along and finally in a good mood.

My friend just bleached her hair.
She looked trashy and we were
stinky from alcohol and smoking in the wind.
We just found out we'd slept with the same exact number of people
and high-fived, happy to know this.

We went to a party and I stared at a girl
with her arm in a cast and then at another,
dressed as a nerd and 4'10" at most,
dancing nasty with a tall blonde with cleavage.
Tall women with cleavage intimidate me.

I was at a party the week before that with a friend dressed as a hooker.
Her tits were at eye level and I sipped my tallboy
and couldn't stop looking at them.
I told her so and we laughed and I'd avert my eyes
but they kept going back.

I went to a show earlier that same night and saw, by surprise,
a rock star I made out with two years ago.
We stood outside and stared hard at a girl riding by on her bike.
She wore a miniskirt and her bare legs pumped the pedals.
I thought, damn, it's kinda cold for that.

My rock star said, *Hey,*
don't you feel like some ogling construction worker?
Just watching girls pass by.
And I can't help from looking.
I can't either.

Between songs she said, *Why live here when it gets so cold?*
Because it's really beautiful in winter, I want to say,
snow falling, being inside (I like being home),
drinking warm drinks.
How bright it gets when sunlight reflects off snow.
People breathing visibly.

She didn't go home with me that night—
not that I was expecting it.
She'll be back in a month, on tour with her other band,
and asked to stay with me in my little apartment—sure!
She's back on the road.

But I also hate it here.
I say it all the time now, without thinking why.
I'm moving when I graduate, tell my rock star so,
tell everyone so.
I'll go somewhere snow won't fall,
no more slush in my shoes, sog on my clothes,
falls on my ass, shoveling till my lungs hurt.

Today mom calls, asks me to evict the guy who lives in front.
Say it strict, she says, and I'm tired, I don't want to.
He lost his job, hasn't paid rent this month,
won't pick up his phone, turn on his lights, open his shades.
I come home and smell cigarette smoke in the hall
and know it's him.

Halloween is in two days.
I will be in class, then work (selling getups that come with thongs),
most likely tired from my yesterday at a basement bar,
where I watched friends sing hard in costume,
while I will look like I always look,
looking at girls,
and not dancing.

NICK MOUDRY

WITH HIS GUN

If Barry Hannah can see Jesus then I
should be able to write a decent poem.
It is 9:51 A.M. like it was the last time
I wrote a poem. Get up, eat breakfast,

read a little, write a poem. How boring
life is & poetry I feel like a factory worker.
It is 9:57 the poem is coming along well
no thought involved, no love.

I have been sick exactly one week & it
is so damn beautiful outside John Wieners
is dead he is not enjoying the weather

either. Tomorrow you will take a trip,
but it will only be to Boston
to see another damn poetry reading.

THEN THE BOMBS

Then there were days of the week when we were allowed to love
Then we loved sometimes but not all the time & when we did our love was such
    incredible love
Then there was love & death & today the weather matched how we felt
Then love & death were only words & were used in the same sentence
Then love is like waking up with a can of Spam in a desert & finding out an
    insurance neophyte & the H-bomb dictated Mecca
Then every time you fly by I think of you up there in the plane & smiling or not
    smiling depending upon the weather
Then the desert gets cold at night when there is no more insurance & you are flying
Then you are flying over our heads & through the fog & also past the mountains &
    the desert
Then there is no more insurance & the weather on land more exactly matches our
    feelings & there is no such thing as death when we are thinking of love
Then life is something we've invented & in our house there are too many breakable
    things such as plants & little glass balls
Then the bombs turn the desert into glass & we can feel it in California & also in
    Massachusetts
Then in Massachusetts the weather suits our feelings clouded by smoke from the
    bombs & would we feel the same in Chicago where it is always cold
Then we will do the same thing over & over & call it a movie
Then we will be in Boston & hear, "John Wieners died this morning" & the weather
    should more exactly match how we feel
Then we will do the same thing over & over & call it a movie
Then John Wieners is dead & every ten seconds there are bombs in the desert & we
    are in Massachusetts loving the indoors & the fog
Then the parties will not be fun & we will come home early
Then there are many poems about love & you are flying overhead in the plane
    carrying the H-bomb
Then the H-bomb was dropped somewhere in Boston & we are in Cambridge &
    also you are flying through the rain & sometimes there is fog
Then it is OK to floss your teeth in the headlights while the bombs are exploding in
    Cambridge
Then from below the desert looks like glass & in looking up you can tell that you are
    not yet buried

LEWIS WARSH

MILTON STREET

1

Before you were born
poets subscribed to light

& later I saw the same
light come up over the street

where lovers cross
over to where the light
stops & starts

the light of conviction
in a stranger's eyes

an unfamiliar voice
on the other end of the line

It sounds like someone died, Bernadette says

2

Not a person, but a depression:
is there a difference? My friends
are my raiments & claim insistence
for my health, which (according
to Plato, not her or him) some toxic
substance endears me to write

So I'll sing not of what love means
but getting older only seems like
love if two people meet on the
other side

As if someone died, & in my desire
disappeared, swallowed up (alive)
for the sake of conviction—it's
always more convenient to die & return
to life, to accept the limits of

resistance (undefined)—& delete

erase her name, as if 'from my life'—
a spark of life went out
before its time

3

I thought I was burned out but I kept
on dreaming. Something revived inside me
that had already died. In my chest still
breathing passed out of my life, like the day
we heard Ted died & fucked all
night. It was the only way we could feel
alive, & keep on breathing, a wedge
between living & dying & eventually we died—
passing to the other side so we could
be with him.

4

I had a plan, more like an overview,
& see what happened. I'd love everybody
at the same time & if they didn't
like it—I'd see who was strong enough,
who was still left standing—

Ping, pounding her chest, says: you have to think
of yourself, also—

As if to remind me what I knew was
true—the baby on the bed, the song

about 'hope' that turned into
sorrow

I had a plan to plagiarize (as if
there was no tomorrow) what others had
said about love's insistence, but I
knew I had the field to myself—the
disparity between what others felt
& their resistance to thinking

what was left in the mind could make
it true

TODD DIEDERICH

There was a time-
   when my voice meant   something.
Through windows,   on the edges of sewers
as we watch   them wash   our dishes.
They wonder-
"where are your painted nails,
your apron and your intrinsic love   of   the   house."
Sitting in here, in a classroom,
with a suit case and the rest of the world.

("I never thought about windows before")

Duct tape across eulogies,
making sundials with pictures-
                  of   all   our   girls.
We wait for midnight.
Curse our tongues   hold our breath
and boy how do we love   to black   out.
In the background-
        wet streets   kiss tires,
and from here,   where do you wake up?
A bed, under a husband, a prison   outside of language?

Hopefully-
someone can hear   morose code.
Tell them, about the silver air
and dents - he called masterpieces
Esther Greenwood
       can't kiss me in traffic now.
But a letter can prove-
that we lost
all   our   girls.

SCOTT KEENEY

FROM *PICKPOCKET POETICA*

Word Problem (for Ron Padgett)

1. None of us really knows what to write
   as we watch the pus gathering around heaven
   sores opening where clouds once were,
   but the thing is we are given
2. A kind of lukewarm craziness of heart.

after Otomo No Yakamochi (718-785)

Law and Order over,
I turn off the light and wait
for sleep's fur-lined cuffs.

The Individual Talent

So as not to wear my feelings on my sleeve
I slipped into my objective correlative shoes.
They suitably contained all that I felt or believed
But inside I was singing the hollow man blues.

A Relationship

Bing! goes the mircrowave.

"Your coffee's done."

"It's not coffee, it's carrots."

SUSEN JAMES

FROM *MY LIFE WITH CHANDELIERS*

LULU

The carpet suffered the most during Lulu's depressive periods. Her obsessive muttering. The continuous soliloquies punctuated with a caustic footstamp. Her pacing. The crushing weight of her plodding steps. Her shuffling. The electrical sparks emitted from the contact of stockinged feet & wool fiber. The occasional flicker of flame. Lulu's saliva rubbed in roughly to extinguish it. And the stains of blood & other body fluids, she'd cover with the ill-mannered & throbbing thud of furniture thrust to obscure its existence. It is no wonder the carpet had to assume control. Pulling from the tiny nails holding it to place, it undulated toward Lulu, waves from each corner of the room. The carpet enclosed her, it embraced her warmly until she remained quiet, until she remained still.

ANTONIO'S RECENT DISCOVERY: A BRIEF SYNOPSES

A quick poke with an exposed electrical wire will wake the recently dead. You must prick them within fifteen minutes of demise before they've had time to bacterially decay. They give a sharp spasm & an enormous mooing sigh. A nacreous cloud will float from their mouths. For the next half hour they'll have the opportunity to say all the things they meant to say, before passing over. This phenomena works only once per corpse. Repeated proddings do nothing except leave electrical burns on the body. It is most beneficial to be there at the exact moment of death, so immediate action can be taken. In a pinch, a knife placed in their hand & thrust into a toaster turned to the highest temperature will supply enough shock.

CONNIE DEANOVICH

HAMLET

His gowns dangle by wires
and his speeches shake inside maracas

His many heads
the many heads of many actors
float through history like elderly hurricanes
whose names no one recalls

Sometimes he crouches like a lithe librarian
then up he comes with knowledge

By this I mean the skull, of course
that big, neckless scene stealer
at which it's healthier to laugh

Sometimes he wears bullfighter's sandals
and hisses the famous venom

This is only when he's revived
taken out of his tottering trunk
to waft and billow
rise and swell
and then once more
to be borne along

ELIXIR

crochet cap

     mumsy

        hussy

SEAN R SLIVE

UNTITLED, UNDATED

In conspiracy, Alain Locke staring back

and then do you know what was said?

it is already saying

kindred in his preciousness

a real educated pussy.

*

A fleshy caring back

a single figure scratched into

marble   an imperfect beige

a distinct trace of gray.

*

The right elbow rests on the knee

this the heart shape

                                        to

                    incite negative space

            *

                    Rising from the base

                        the sex of the figure

            in tangible flux

                ménage a quâtre

    (the thumb, perhaps the pinky)

    how do you know that girl?

                    I have not seen her dance

    or even her lips.

*

Transcribed onto fleshy hips

eyelids and buttocks

must look closely

at the back

upper buttocks, arms and face

all of which are visible in this

fragment

a prying (re: political) inquisition

the intimation

'golden lotuses'

with(in) *outsider.*

D.J. DOLACK

GROCERY LIST

1.
I only wish to be as close to you
as the weather, where you don't
understand not feeling.

2.
Her whistling lit a canary on fire
            as it sat in a tree, perplexed.
Her lips: the metaphor to which
we owe our partition.

3.
Gravity was never looking up when it smoked.

4.
The critters in your apartment give you
all my names;
                  those not yet even spoken.

5.
Sometimes there's a gag order on
your voice
and I'm scared of what you'll call me.

6.
I write my love note on her napkin: Dear
        Lover, I write this
                  on a napkin . . . —etc. and so on.

KIM HAYES

GOING AROUND

misplacing the heart   is no worse than a dinner party   souffle falling into   abstraction   who stitched
these embroidered napkins   and fundamentalists by hand   anyway all stains   are not blind spots and
well-earned   work-like-a-dog was his   version of putting on the veil   he bathed these children of god
too with warm washcloths   and a mouthful of thorns   take small steps toward   modernism when a
camera moves close to your   great oceans she said to me   polls show they've been   praying more and
never   leaving the house a bad   imitation of western   and I'm going around on one side   lately had no
food   shy in these tiny circles   most of the faces are   waving flags   putting on the nightlight   as
winter approaches   is extremist eight months ago   husbands knock on the door wanting   the majority
of women   don't have to lose two or three   pounds to absorb what's going on   that's a very important
thing to say   outdoors   these days   with a little stick

THE LIGHT IS JUST

right today.   as indefinable and crisp as the future
thus defined as the infinity of possibilities

other words for crisp are: green, plump, fresh, vigor
it is morning, of course.   the only time to list

the greatest human virtues   meanwhile and as per usual
the house is imitating a bad cold.   influenza-ing

because this hierarchy corresponds to the order of
universal temporality like fidelity and loyalty

and the house is spreading, but don't worry.   don't
ever worry. every person I know has trouble

writing. has trouble. *for who hast not in thy brow*
an eye discerning thine honor from thy suffering?

don't get me wrong here, I love all the seasons
the mixing and the quarreling.   the whole

existence of man tearing things apart.   just try
to pay attention to the ballet itself and its shadow

other words for beauty are: our hopes tied in hoops
there on the bushes.   transforming pod into a religious

question.   and the trees.   how each tree touches
something the body. they are shapes. trees

symbolize growth and wanting a child and wanting
and being childish. wanting to swing.   to give

all that is unspeakable. what the tree says to the body
if the body is like the tree it won't have to go far

for what it needs. you are lucky because your
parents actually understand all this.   have never

been bored.   another word for lucky is unusual
and whatever errors are committed by the advocates

of piecemeal reform, regard equality.   even cleaning
can be fun on a morning like this.   or not cleaning

not cleaning is fine too.   because I grew very excited
thinking of knowing you.   the complete unknown

of you.   and poof, just like that, an extraordinary
new space opens up in my little world.   which is love

ARIELLE GREENBERG

MY SISTER TAKES ON THE CLOTHING OF THE DEAD

Tenderly, possums leak out like a necklace from a burrow—
it's actually really gross, how nakedly they skim each other for their sight,
their beating, bolted parts. They chirp like cicadas to plot the course.
And did you know that on some continents as yet unmapped,
there's a kind of animal that keeps its young in a big wet pocket lined with
    snot? A zoo
is a horrible place, because once a snake or a diamond-back panther
sheds its skin, they film it and then reuse the dermis for another person from
    a warmer clime,
like a llama, who is stupid and doesn't know better, and then they distribute
    the film
as porn. Each armpit is encoded with an invisible plastic strip so you know
    who's who.
Each porn name is glommed from the genus like a scab: for instance,
panda (which is not a bear at all) would be called *Miss Ailuri Melano*,
    please welcome her to our stage.
Each overcoat you buy at the thrift store to wear on the safari tour bus
smells like the closets of an dirty trainer whose bad habits lead
to the untoward cultish killings by a pride of lions under cover of day, in
    housedress.
 So while yes, that is a pretty skirt, it was probably not meant for folk
    dancing.

Shh—listen—the gazelles are singing the backwards of your Latin name.

LITTLE RED FOX

Yeah, it'll chomp you. It does like meat.
It likes your leg. It looks so sweet. It looks like rain,
so cancel the invitations—if you throw a soiree,
the woodchuck will chomp you with its twisted
Indian name. So will the set of wolverine teeth,
unabated. So will the tribe—they're pretty pissed.
You thought you would escape the rats
but here you are, a groom
at the rat-wedding, tying down the wet horses.
It's now your job, not your colony.
You're the most eligible bachelor the new world has seen.
Such creatures, such fucked-up land.
Every bride's a hailstorm, every mammal
with a back jaw that unlocks runs
through woods. Did you know the sign of
carnivore, how it backs its arrow in the stars?
The rats are lovely tonight, moonless.
Dark and deep. But you look a bit owlish to me.
The voice of the branches with their death
coming out—that will chomp you.
That sounds like several maids of honor at once,
all sewn together in their matching gowns,
their long, thin tails, their Indian names, their prey.

ARTURO ALMAZAN

WALL BASH

the clock desper-
ate to turn
with mr.
biggs and jonny
littles. one
workshop to go
until the old
school teacher
missing two
fingers run out
of space to
write on the
blackboard.

He wears black
to outline his
complexion and
coughs from the
dust that sits
on his hands.
a dream told
me he wore black
out of respect
for his par-
ents carried his
face with his
feet in his
pockets because
of the dis-
comfort.

The loop poured
out bobbeggers
grasping dunk-
in donut cups.
trumpets blaze

near corner
lights.
Heavy coats
roam the area
and hats decorate
stop signs.
taxis sound
yellow with
a spin
of comic shows.

jitter fingers
flicker for a
couple of minutes
keeping company
the flashy man
laying on the
watery curb.
steps are
obstacles to
climb the magic
bus and pass
thru the jungle.

close-ups with
workers dealing
drugs under
their parents front
porch. tumble
with clowns
potrayed as
business men
on monday
morning.

KATHLEEN GARDNER

GOING TO WORK IN HIS PAJAMAS

there are two elevator bays that
never meet.

because of this
I have never been to the ninth floor
which is a feeling that presses into
my back like a nail into a soft piece
of fruit or when I'm face first
in his neck and have to bite the part
of his shoulder that is always up far
enough to block half the window like a real mountain on a glass horizon

it's too depressing to think about.
I will not win the italian man dressed
like this

I tell
him I always
found him annoying and
that's why I wanted to draw him
with big

lobster
claws and that's why
I was drinking so much
I was always hammered around
him and

I tell
him that he's so
fucking hot that his dick
could be my curling iron and
I'm drunk

when I
tell him I love
him I'm so wasted and
its an accident on the Dan
Ryan

that kills
a family of
five and backs up traffic
for fucking hours and it's on
the news

and I'm
plastered when I
say it and it falls like
wet moldy laundry over both
of us

and I
can't take it back
and he gives me the speech
on why he likes me for the same
reasons

he likes
other peoples'
pets and I can hear the
fire detector beeping in
the hall

because
the battery
is low and it reminds
me every fifteen minutes all
night it

reminds
me that I'm not
burning up but there's a
possibility I will be
if I

insist
on being too
lazy to replace it
and every motherfucking night
I think

shut the
hell up I'll do
it tomorrow and then
I think about the two things I
would take

if my
apartment were
on fire and decide
that I'd grab my rabbit and my
chapstick

ZSOLT SZENTGYORGYI

DISTANT SHORES

above the city the sky
was grey like a dead bride
and oftentimes the birds
perished by loneliness
with tousled feathers
on the street of ice
where the street lights
were on all day long
but the dusk filtered into
the houses under the doors
and the housewives got tired
of washing it up and
they had to put out the kitties
to the backyards
because they made
such a big mess
with their foggy hair.

our life was like living in a hat
and we tried in vain to peep out
we couldn't see its other shore.

QUIET TIMES

the church had a big chimney
which reached up to the sky
almost like the chimney of our factory
but instead of smoke
this one gave out bundles of summer grass
and cows with airplane engines
strapped under their bellies
were flying around up there
in the sunny air
catching a mouthful now and then
and making sweet milk all the time.

NERISSA HAMLIN

there was this girl.
           she was an outfit.
               an outfit!
          I became quite
involved with the stitching
              on the strap of her bag
              an outfit!
much like dental floss scrounging for toys
in a corner. don't worry! it's
only a little blood, not a matter
for pus.
              an outfit!
          like jumprope.
there is this move, this , this,
um,
um, this kind of jumping,
two ropes, an intersection
and oh the shapes they made
                an outfit!
not really like usual, you know,
like a hotdog, but but like the way
a cap looks after it sat all day on the
head of a bald man.

the head of a bald man!

in some places, the head is the toilet,
but not by association. use
this.

Read not like you are in an orchard
plucking apples from trees and saying,
"These are apple trees."

THE FIRST NUDE

forget about the ship
how do you think the water felt
the water felt heavy
burdened by fingers
downward pointed pressing pressure
plucked, blown, and begging
the water was stuffed.

a wax ship in a cup of sand

he made her
from spit in the shower
contraposso, he supposed,

to be the most adhesive
blunted with icing,
like licking the stripe on a straw
all sound is a result of something moving

oh, how

she was carried to the center and surrounded by a fence
and some chairs.

SARA ATKINS

LINEAGE

I am looking for the women of my house.
Your grandmothers and doves and ebony spiders.
We are running out of the glass rooms.
We are all imprisoned in the castles of our skins.

I am looking for the women of my house.
I knew rooms full of ashes.
Am I dressed right for the smoke?
The spells we want to be under
Glow plain and foreign
Sometimes with one I love I fill myself with rage.

I am looking for the women of my house.

You slipped quickly into magic.
Mothers pass,
          Say,
Keep walking though there's no place to get to.
A woman precedes me up the long rope
          Says,
There is only the dance.

I am looking for the women of my house.
The warrior in me returns.
She will cultivate night vision.
          She will follow
The earth into which the path was pressed.
          She will say,
I only borrowed this dust.

ANI GRIGORIAN

REGARDING THE TOMATO PLANTS

God spoilt
that arrangement,

not adapting
the large storm,

that ignorant
droplet's game,

gleaming death
to transport

garden-path
glitter to moans.

Goodnight,
prenatal matters,

potential
grandmother tags.

POEM FOR MY BIRTHMARK

you follow the natural order
of all things living. mother
birthed me and i, you
on the back of my thigh.
brother dubbed you "shit stain"
after his theory on how you came about,
but i adore you, regardless—
such a loyal tenant in my house—
and he who visits with his lips
warms you, worships you,
thinks the cat who dipped
her paw into his coffee cup
went for a stroll on my thigh.
my mellow spot of melanin,
that is how his story goes,
and i allow it to be told.

DENISE DUHAMEL

THE MADONNA IN ME

At least I'm not Madonna, I tell my parents
who are embarrassed by the confessional
nature of my poetry. *At least I don't fake masturbate
on a big peach bed on stage while men in pointy bras
slither around me.* The Madonna in me
wants to tell you every shocking detail,
wants to substitute Oreos for communion,
wants to kiss the Black Christ of Nazareth
while grabbing his ceramic balls. The Madonna in me
wants to own my own company
and put my name brand on everything.
The Madonna in me wants to star
in every movie and have children
but never change a diaper. The Madonna in me
is crazy about yoga and goes swimming
in Rosie's pool. The Madonna in me is afraid
to get old, is afraid she's already gotten too old
to shock people anymore. There is no poet
equivalent of Madonna. There isn't even
a performance-poet equivalent of Madonna
though in *Truth or Dare* Madonna recites
a poem she wrote herself—remember?—
for her assistant's birthday. The Madonna in me
wants Madonna to read my book. The Madonna in me
wants Madonna to casually mention me
in an interview. The Madonna in me wants
Madonna to dress up like me instead of a Geisha.
The Madonna in me is afraid that the real
Madonna is becoming a caricature of herself
and that by the time she does mention my book
in an *Allure* exclusive no one will follow
her good taste. A friend who works at Books and Books
in Coral Gables actually has a copy of a receipt
of Madonna's purchases. He's memorized her visa number
and the titles she bought—coffee table books mostly.
He shows me her signature just to prove
it looks nothing at all like mine.

DAVID TRINIDAD

"I DETEST CHEAP SENTIMENT"

[From *Phoebe 2002: An Essay in Verse,* a collaboration with Jeffery Conway and Lynn Crosbie. *Phoebe 2002* is a mock-epic based on the 1950 movie *All About Eve,* starring Bette Davis as Broadway star Margo Channing. In order to teach Margo a lesson in humility, her best friend Karen Richards (Celeste Holm) drained the gas from their car; the two sit stranded on a wintry country road. Margo will miss her evening performance, allowing her much younger understudy, Eve Harrington, to go on in her place.]

"**I** detest cheap sentiment." So declares Margo,
dryly, clicking "Liebestraum" (the song she couldn't get
enough of two weeks earlier, soused at her soiree) off

the car radio. Also in Mankiewicz's shooting script, but
eliminated from the finished film: Margo's recognition that
she has "an understudy so ready, so willing and so able

to go on." This knowledge is stated "quietly," without
consternation. One thinks of a long chorus line, the
history of cinematic understudies—from Busby Berkeley's

earnest hoofer (Ruby Keeler) to Verhoeven's Vegas viper
(**a** Berkley of a different color). The former is told by the tem-
peramental leading actress (Bebe Daniels) that she has

so much to give the audience: "youth, beauty, freshness."
Ever the trooper, Keeler taps hope into the heart of a
nation deflated by Depression, and comes back a star.

The shifting limbs of Berkeley's human kaleidoscopes, his
innumerable violin- and piano-playing chorus
members, anticipate the infinite mirroring at the

end of *All About Eve.* About our '90s showgirl, well:
no need to wait for the star to run out of gas or
twist her ankle—just push the bitch down the stairs.

ALL ABOUT MIRRORS

[The following scene takes place at the end of the film.]

All about mirrors, a central trope of the movie,
complicated here at the end, a movement fulfilled.
Margo, at her vanity, has demanded the heart
of the young girl; Eve and Karen have sought

recognition in Margo's magic mirror; and now
Phoebe doth behold / Her silver visage in the wat'ry glass.
Like the Lady of Shalott, she weaves by night and day
a web of magic sights: her own ambition, *greatly multiplied.*

I am silver and exact, says the mirror. Phoebe basks in
the perfect silver of [its] reflectiveness. Such a girl has
looked in too many mirrors to experience experience as experience.
The glass chooses to reflect only what she sees, which is

enough for her purpose, the gospel according to Phoebe: *endless
drill team in [her own] likeness,* begotten in perfect formation,
a regiment of Hitler's daughters . . . copies exact in all details,
the girls from Brazil. If we could enter Phoebe's mirror the way

Deckard digitally scans the mirror in Leon's photograph, searching
for hidden clues, what would we find? *Enhance 34 to 46. Pull back.
Wait a minute. Go right. Stop. Enhance 57-19. Track 45 left. Stop.
Enhance 15 to 23.* Eve, the original replicant, passed out on the couch,

left hand draped across one breast. *Give me a hard copy right there.*
Shadows of the world appear. Phoebe *tends the image / she sees
in her glass, / the cold replication / of woman, / the one
who dared eat / from her own hand / the fruit of self-knowledge.*

There is no terminus, says Plath, *only suitcases* [i.e., trunks]
*Out of which the same self unfolds like a suit / Bald and shiny,
with pockets of wishes, / Notions and tickets, short circuits and
folding mirrors.* According to Mankiewicz's script, Phoebe quietly

puts on Eve's "fabulous wrap" and picks up the award. Slowly,
she walks to a large *three*-mirrored cheval. With grace and infinite
dignity she holds the award to her, and bows again and again . . .
as if to the applause of a multitude. According to Robinson Jeffers,

awards, prizes, and ceremony *kill the [wo]man.* Might not the
mirror-panels begin to flap on each side of Phoebe, bird that she is,
like silver wings? And on such wings might she not ascend, a beatific
apparition—nimbus, blue and white robes, rays of light emanating

from the golden award? The Assumption of Phoebe, the "bright one,"
into Heaven. Attended by guns, by roses, by whatever these empyreal things
mean. What is reality to this pure synthetic virgin? *This otherness, this*
"Not-being-us" is all there is to look at / In the mirror, though no one can

say / How it came to be this way. Smoke and mirrors: Karen Weiser calls, at
the end of *Phoebe,* to say she may have discovered, in Richard Klein's *Cigarettes*
Are Sublime, the origin of the "cigarette grisette": *La cigarette est gentille, vive,*
animée; elle a quelquechose de piquant dans ses allures. C'est la grisette
        des fumeurs

(Théodore Burette, 1840). Our Lady of Philip Morris. Our Lady of Blood-Stained
Roses. Our Lady of Borrowed Light. The three of us firing at each other in the
Magic Mirror Maze: *One who follows his nature keeps his original nature*
in the end. The Mirror Crack'd (one of Liz's worst) from side to side. Shattered—

the Pleasures of Peace. Bomb blasts in Bali, the Philippines, Northern Israel.
Sniper shots in Kuwait and Washington, D.C.
                        And now the end of something—

Our Lady of the Paused DVD, expiring amongst spent cartridges and silver
        shards.

Works Cited

William Shakespeare, *A Midsummer Night's Dream*
Sylvia Plath, "Mirror"
James Merrill, "Mirror"
Rosmarie Waldrop, *Split Infinites*
John Ashbery, "Self-Portrait in a Convex Mirror"
Jeffery Conway, *Chain Chain Chain*
Alfred, Lord Tennyson, "The Lady of Shalott"
Kathryn Stripling Byer, "Vanity"
Sylvia Plath, "Totem"
Sylvia Plath, "Fever 103°"
Anne Sexton, "Self in 1958"
The Lady from Shanghai (movie), 1948

JORIS SOEDING

ONE MORE SUNDAY

Well, this is it
one more Sunday
one more teaser followed
by the theme followed
by the arguments believer and
non-believer followed
by the case solved
or un-
solved

FERD EGGAN

FROM THE JAPANESE [1]

Power from perineum, anus sigmoid colon, narrowing.

Curvaceous intestines whirling empty center.
Above and below a line in space, a
Big nose bald headed guy in a
Funky wheelchair was pulled by a cat.
He used
Infinity or opera glasses
to look at a duck far away
or small in his view.
Ignatz the mouse of Krazy Kat
found himself praying
To the wheeled god,
leaning back on his tail.

Far away, an African stood tall with a head bundle, above his head
Cobra light bulbs flashing an idea repetitiously,
A shorter African became a vulture and
Conversed with a short emphatic snake with a dotted rattle.
On the roof, a witch or elf
Slid dangerously on the leftward slope
as earth broke apart and magma flowed from deep crevices hiccupping upward.

Jesus up there above the line had a good view, Mary was crouching, wishing
    she could get near a
little fire on the right.
A robber, not as bold, was sagging as his bowels loosened and made a pool
    at the bottom of his cross. A Romany duck or St. Paul strutted unaware,
    resplendent,
Toward the other thief (who might be Jesus again, but slightly less empha-
    sized in the
picture).

Again, power from perineum, anus colon narrowing to a symbolizing
    emptiness of intestines.

The hatted man now walked with a crutch and carried a baby
To a frantic mother who rushed up, hair flying, dress open, exposing her
    breasts and sex,
While at the river a boat discharged a foppish official with too many angles.

Suddenly, a candle guttered, or maybe it was a perfunctory human interro-
    gating in brutal boots,
torturing a quivering human frightened by the violent, sneering officer.
The official flaunted vampirish eyebrows above a scarred and punishing
    face, winking
At his aristocratic chief with a sinister half smile.

Then, oddly, a sailor stole a schooner, another sailor stole another schooner,
    watched by a
Very complex woman, vain but coy, flirtatious on chunky heels, walking
    away in disdain.
One sailor cried as the ship sailed away.

---

1 Unknown, printed in *Tricycle*, December 2002.

THE POETRY SCHOLARSHIP FUND

The English Department of Columbia College Chicago is pleased to have received the following donations to its Poetry Scholarship Fund. The initial goal of the fund is to raise $20,000 to provide an annual scholarship of $1,000 for a deserving student in the college's undergraduate poetry major. Columbia College Chicago is the only institution of higher learning in the country to offer an undergraduate poetry major, which consists of 51 semester hours of study. Further gifts are welcome and should be addressed to:

> The Poetry Scholarship Fund
> College Relations & Development Office
> 600 South Michigan Avenue
> Chicago, IL 60605-9988

Contribution of $2000+:
Anonymous

Contribution of $1,000-$1,999:
Michelle M. McCart
The Chicago Literary Club

Contribution of $500-$999:
Garnett Kilberg-Cohen
Elaine Sorkin in memory of David G. Sorkin

Contribution of $349-$499:
Karen Lee Osborne and JoAnn E. Ziebarth

Contribution of $250-$349:
Bank One Chicago
Sharon Darrow
Elizabeth Shepherd
Vincent A. Rosenthal

Contribution of $150-$249:
Susan K. Anzaldi
Paul Hoover
Cheryl Johnson-Odim
Don B. Klugman
Art Lange

Contribution of $100-$149:
Anonymous
Charles E. Cannon
Mark E. Kelly
Donald E. Osborne

Contribution of $50-$99:
Steven A. Bithos
Suzanne Blum Malley
Mitchell A. Newman
Tony Trigilio and Shelly Hubman

Contribution of $10-$49:
Jennifer Brookmeyer
Deckard Hodge
Phyllis Nelson
Alexis Sarkisian
Jana Tuzar
Mary L. Wade